Beauty Is In The Eyes Of The Beholder!

Seydali Mesut

Lulu Books

The Worlds Best Books

Once upon a time, there was a woman named Megan. By all definitions Megan was the physical embodiment of beauty and had always been. While still nestled in her mother's womb, she was constantly reminded of her beauty; her mother would sing her songs that proclaimed just how beautiful a child she would be and tell everyone that would listen, how perfect a child was expected.

On the day of her birth, Megan was taken from the delivery room to the hospital's nursery and all the nurses were astonished by her beauty. She had long eyelashes, perfect hands and feet and even then, a beautiful body. People in the adjacent waiting room would peer through the glass picture windows and comment on the beautiful new baby, often bypassing their own new born for a chance to look at baby Megan.

Once home, Megan was the center of the family's attention. She was said to be the perfect baby in every way, even her doctor noted that Megan was exceptional. But it wasn't too long before Megan's parents noticed an annoying little personality flaw, for even as an infant, Megan was extremely demanding and would raise the roof with her cry when things were not going exactly her way. But that was such a small price for her parent's to pay for such a perfect baby.

Megan was extremely bright, they would marvel. At an exceeding young age she mastered a significant vocabulary. When waking, she would bellow, "Juice" to everyone in ear shot, when other toddlers her age would barely be able to say Momma or Papa, two words that Megan rarely uttered, except to direct her orders. She was extremely fussy and spared no time in saying what she disliked. Most green vegetables were simply, "Yuck" to Megan. When offering ice cream her family soon learned it had to be "Nilla," or nothing at all. Strawberry was a flavor chosen only if the offending adult wished to wear it! But Megan was beautiful and everyone still told her so.

This was pretty much Megan's life until she turned four, when Momma decided at her pediatrician's prompting, that it was time for Megan to develop her social skills and go to pre-school.

This was a big change for little Megan, who up to this point had the run of the house at home and everyone waiting on her every whim. Pre-school was a different experience, but in her own, already developing style, Megan set out to change the system, no matter what the price.

Megan's first day at pre-school orientation was a trend setter for the next year. Momma was told to simply leave Megan at the doorway to the classroom and leave. This in itself was difficult for both Momma and Megan. Momma had always been there, by her side and at her beckoned call. "Just drop her off?" Momma was near hysteria's door by the time she reached Classroom # 4, the four year olds domain. In spite of her misgivings, she pointed Megan in the direction of a group of age appropriate kids in the classroom and as instructed, turned to leave.

"Momma," Megan shouted. "Stay!"

The tone was not one of a child apprehensive about her new environment, it was one might use when addressing a puppy! Megan had the drill down pat. Momma was her slave and Momma had not been dismissed. This potentially ugly scene was interrupted by Miss Christina, a young, attractive teacher with long auburn hair, much like Megan's, kind eyes and knowing smile. Momma noted that the young teacher was about her age, but certainly more in control than she could ever be. "It's OK. You can leave…" she told Momma, glancing back over her shoulder with one eye on her new charge. "I've got it under control." she added.

Momma seems stuck to the floor boards outside classroom #4. She heard what the young woman had said, but looked instinctively to the four year old for further direction. Miss Christina motioned to the directress of the school knowingly and a short, Asian woman came to take Momma away by the arm.

"Momma!" Megan shouted out in a firm directive tone, much like you might when that new puppy failed to follow your directive.

Miss Christina stood between the doorway and Megan, anticipating the child's next move and move she did, like a linebacker with an eye toward finding a weakness in the opposition's defenses.

"Nope," Miss Christina said with a friendly smile, fending off a frontal assault that a Prussian General would have been proud of by Megan. "Sorry, honey, but you have to stay here and Mommy has to leave."

Megan stalled in her offensive for a moment. Who was this woman who thought she could tell the all powerful Megan what to do. Didn't she know that it was Megan who always made the rules? Megan then made another lunge for the doorway, screaming, "Momma, Momma!" this time with a touch of urgency in her tone. But Momma was already safely in the Director's office, being taught the Montessori way of handling a child.

"Please understand, we offered your daughter a scholarship based on her testing scores, but you have to understand we have our methods," the Director explained to Mamma. "We offer your child the best learning environment possible and her teacher, Miss Christina is fully certified to deal with even the most unruly child," she explained in a monotone voice. Momma was apprehensive. Miss Christina was perhaps in her early twenties and surely not prepared for her daughter. Momma was wrong!

Back in the classroom, there was no time for a stand-off, which was Megan's original plan. Miss Christina was not going to have any of that and she was obviously one step ahead of Momma when it came to tactics. Miss Christina had at her disposal a phalanx of already brainwashed four year olds on hand to deal directly with the obstinate newcomer, and Megan quickly realized she was entering an entirely new field of combat, that would require much more subtle measures than she ever needed at home with her own family. She quickly came to understand that she was in the presence of seven kids her own age, each with their own hidden agenda.

For whatever reason, Megan liked the idea of this new challenge and at least for the present would comply with the attractive Miss Christina and her peers until she could hatch a better plan.

Preschool was structured, something that Megan had never encountered before, but which she could easily manipulate to her own interests, she reckoned. How could a handful of kids be any match for her, the little princess of adult manipulation? Miss Christina, on the other hand, might be more of a challenge, but Megan figured it would not take long to find her weaknesses too, and learn to manipulate them as well. She was wrong on both counts, in fact, a new world was opening up for Megan, a new set of challenges and skills were to be called for, which eventually would serve this young beauty for the next twenty years.

Miss Christina was actually a college graduate student, who was Montessori certified with a background in early childhood development and working with "special needs' children, who had come to Megan's new school to fit in to her college schedule. If Megan had been assigned to any other classroom, her task would have been far less daunting, but Miss Christina was going to be a real challenge for "the princess," as her teacher would soon refer to her. In fact, from the first moment they met, Miss Christina knew that little Megan would become her choice for a case study she was working on for her post graduate degree, which would make Megan's task all the more difficult. Once the center of a course study, Miss Christina would never surrender willingly to this precocious four year old, but of course, Megan didn't know that at the time.

But while Megan didn't realize it yet, she would learn more about behavior modification from Miss Christina than she would ever need in her adult life, tools that would make the manipulation of those who she encountered in the future literally child's play. The next few months would be a challenge, but more than rewarding for both of these combatants.

Miss Christina was surprised at just how easily Megan fell into the mold after their initial encounter on her first day in class.

Megan turned out to be the model student, except of course, for the fact that she easily manipulated all of her classmates and several of the staff members at the school. Miss Christina was modifying Megan's responses, but Megan was in turn using every one of those tactics to control the rest of the players in this pre-school version of real life.

Megan easily learned the jargon of early childhood development. "Megan, we don't do it that way. You must share," Miss Christina, would say in a loving, parenting tone, and Megan would comply. But out of the teacher's earshot, Megan would then use those same tools on her classmates. Want a certain toy, but Billy already has it? "Share and share alike, Billy. That is what Miss Christina says!" would be Megan's response. The fact that her vocabulary and articulation was so far advanced over her peers made it all simple for, "The Princess." And Miss Christina didn't object.

In the beginning, Miss Christina was running on remote control, so to speak. She was busy with her own college work, all the necessary paperwork at the pre-school and of course a personal life, which would soon be drawn into Megan's web of influence. Megan was nothing, if not observant. She watched and waited for her opportunities, much like a lion stalking its prey. To Megan, this was a wonderful game, there was so much more to learn, so many new methods to be tried out in her own world. In some ways, Megan was not just mastering pre-school, but learning the lessons needed to master the world in general. She was already a master of manipulation, but her skills were reaching new heights and she was quickly learning how to accomplish her goals with a minimum or fuss and usually under most adults' radar.

Megan watched Miss Christina, not just when she was working with the other children or herself, but with the staff members, supervisors and later, with her boyfriend. What a wonderful opportunity. Much better than back home where Momma was just not a challenge anymore.

Megan was learning new skills with each passing day., not just how to get a toy she wanted from a classmate, but more rewarding skills, for instance how to get an extra cookie at snack time from the kitchen helper or how to guarantee that Vanilla ice cream would always be available, without throwing the obvious tantrum. This was so much more rewarding than the old ways of getting what you wanted by sheer will, for Megan it was as easy as falling off a log; so simple it would make your mind spin.

At home, of course Megan knew it was best to continue to use her old tactics, lest the family figure out her game plan for future conquests. But Megan soon was using more than her good looks to get what she wanted, yes her beauty was her greatest asset, but she was soon learning that her intellect was also equal to the task. Brains and good looks would make her invincible.

Megan was an excellent observer. She could size up a situation at age four the way that a seasoned detective might hope to at 40 and she did it without being noticed most of the time. One day, she saw Miss Christina by the fence during afternoon playtime at the rear of the school. She was talking to a young man, very tall, Megan thought. Megan walked over after first throwing a ball in the general direction where her two targets were standing. First she got the ball and had an opportunity to listen for a moment to the conversation without either her teacher or friend noticing her. Then she approached the pair with a smile.

"Hi, I'm Megan," she said to the man on the other side of the fence.

"Hello, I'm Roy," the man responded.

"Megan is one of my students," Miss Christina added to the conversation, at the same time motioning to Megan that she should rejoin the class.

"Are you Miss Christina's boyfriend?" Megan quickly asked.

"Well, ah…." The man stammered in response.

"Well, you know you should marry her or you'll probably loose her," Megan added.

"Megan, go back to the class," the teacher requested softly.

"Well, it's true! You're too pretty for him, anyway!" she answered, skipping off in the general direction of her classmates. Adding as she turned, "Bye. Nice meeting you!"

"Boy, was that a kid or a midget," the young man quickly asked.

"She is precocious, but yeah, she is only four," Miss Christina responded.

"Four going on 40, I think!" The young man added. "I gotta go and leave you to your prodigy over there," the man noted as he headed toward the parking lot.

This was a typical Megan move and not without some purpose in mind. Megan was beginning to really enjoy playing with other people's heads. Her mind was like a steel trap, she would file away everything she learned for future use. She was totally dedicated to her game and always enjoyed the outcomes, whether she was dropping a hint at the breakfast table that Papa smelled of perfume when he got in late last night, or telling Miss Christina how pretty she was. Everything had a purpose in her little life, far from the norm for most kids her age. She always had an agenda.

In school, her relationships with classmates were typical of this mind bending play. Megan had an excellent vocabulary and used it to belittle her classmates without ever suggesting they were less than her closest friends. While the slower of her classmates would simply ignore this, the smarter ones knew there was something hurtful inside Megan, although they certainly could not verbalize it to their teacher or parents.

Miss Christina had already decided to use Megan for a course "project" but needed to interview her parents, who readily agreed to talk about their little darling. Of course, Miss Christina was not a seasoned interviewer and if there were any deep secrets in the family closet, they were not about to divulge them, on the surface, at least, they had the perfect child and would go to the grave saying so.

On the day that Miss Christina came to visit, a Saturday afternoon, Momma and Papa were with Megan in the living room, just as Megan wanted it. After the niceties, the group sat down, iced tea on hand and Miss Christina pulled out a notebook. First the basics, information about the birth, Megan was an only child, all the nurses said how beautiful she was, even when she was hours old, Momma noted with pride.

Papa was a day laborer and far less chatty, he answered Miss Christina's questions frankly and honestly but added little to the conversation. Miss Christina did notice that Papa had dark black hair, long and strait, Momma brown and close cropped, while Megan had a deep Auburn set of locks, much like her teachers, which were naturally curly and fell to the middle of her back. Megan, Miss Christina noted, was an odd match for her parents, although they reiterated stories about the birth, even while the teacher thought the child seemed more like an adoptee who had been ill fitted to her new genetic environment.

Neither parent was nearly as articulate as Megan and the teacher felt it was important to ask how that came to be. Momma said proudly, "Oh, she watches a great deal of TV."

"You mean educational TV, like PBS," Miss Christian asked.

"Oh no, she has been watching the soaps with me since she came home from the hospital. She would listen intently and when she first began speaking, it was usually about the characters she was watching on the tube," Momma responded.

Miss Christina was astonished. She had come to visit expecting something totally different. Here was an exceptional child, bright, beautiful and articulate living in a neat enough lower middle class environment and seeming totally out of place. She didn't look like either of her parents, she had already surpassed them in many ways and the teacher had no idea how she might have matured so quickly.

During a later discussion with her own class advisor in psychology, Christina raised several of these issues and at first, had her concerns dismissed by the grad student she was talking with. Later, when she presented her paper to the professor, she was invited to visit with her instructor and two other faculty members.

At that meeting, the trio asked more pointed questions of the young graduate teacher; where did she get her material, was there really a Megan, was her data fully truthful and accurate. Miss Christina was taken aback. Of course there as such a child, she assured the instructors, she was a student in her pre-school whom she worked with every day and of course, all the notes were accurate. The faculty members seemed both astonished and doubtful.

"Surely, you read some case notes in abnormal psych that has colored your report on this child," one older teacher suggested.

"But I haven't taken abnormal psych yet. The class was closed out this year before I registered," Miss Christina argued. "Why? What is going on?" she asked the men.

"Well you have done an excellent job of reporting what has to be a classic case of abnormal behavior in a pre-schooler, if all of your facts are correct," one man offered.

"But," Miss Christina protested. "It is all true. Every word of it. I recognized that Megan was an exceptional child from the first day."

The three instructors continued their questions, a day by day recollection of everything the young teacher could remember about her illustrious charge. They took notes on everything, from how Megan had reacted on the first day of school until her last encounter the day previous. When they were finished, they were the ones who were left open-mouthed. They told Miss Christina that they wished to meet with Megan at the pre-school and told her to advise the school director that they would be in touch.

"But why," the young teacher asked. "Megan is not abused or neglected. She is the perfect little girl, very bright. A bit overpowering to many, but that is just because she is so much brighter than the people she encounters...." Miss Christina protested.

"My dear, you have done a wonderful job of reporting a most unusual phenomenon here. No doubt you have earned an "A" for your class work and you might even see some of your research in a journal article some day, but you are also out of your depth in this case study, you have stumbled into something that is very rare and we will have to ask you to cooperate with us on this one," the professor said with a very strong look of consternation on his face.

Miss Christina agreed to talk with her administrator about a visit and left the office both pleased with the outcome, her "A" and still a bit confused as to what the academics were seeing in her paper that she was overlooking.

When Miss Christina mentioned the planned visitation by her university's faculty members to her director, she was pleased, but also a bit confused as to what had prompted their interest. Miss Christina gave a copy of her paper to her superior and later that day, the older woman said that she had read it and was still clueless as to what the academics were seeing, but that naturally, they were welcome to come and observe their now prized student.

Back in class, everything seemed normal. Megan was still her old self, but now Miss Christina was more likely to observe the subtleties of her behavior and interaction with the other students. Over the next week, she became more aware of how Megan could, and always did, manipulate any situation to her best advantage. A four year old who could manipulate her peers, both verbally and amazingly, with great psychological acumen. From getting the toy she wanted or her favorite spot in the sand box, to controlling the flow of nap time as she desired. Once aware of it, Miss Christina realized just how unique a child Megan really was and finally came to the conclusion that precocious was not a good enough title for her charge.

Whether Megan was aware of these subtle changes in her teacher was debatable, but if she was, she certainly wasn't concerned. In fact, if anything she was becoming more aggressive in her personal connection with her teacher, a fact that came into the spotlight one afternoon when Roy returned to the school for a quick lunchtime visit with his girlfriend.

Running into the four year old in the hallway outside the classroom, Megan immediately addressed him by name, a very unusual occurrence for a child so young and a chance meeting for only a minute several months before.

"Did you ask her to marry you, yet?" Megan asked abruptly.

"Well, no I haven't," the young man responded.

"Just as well. I really don't like you all that much, anyway," Megan concluded, never missing a step as she joined the line to go back to class.

Shocked, Roy immediately reported the incident to Miss Christina, who immediately saw a pattern she would have otherwise overlooked. Megan, who had gained a reputation for being extremely short with adults at the school, was always polite and chatty with her teacher. Megan's remarkable recall and short interchange with Miss Christina's boyfriend seemed just one more piece in the puzzle, which she in turn mentioned to her professor at the school that evening.

Within a week, each of the professors involved in the original meeting with Miss Christina had come to the school to observe Megan and each was shocked at what they found. In turn Megan was more aware now of the scrutiny she was under and began to react. She told her mother that strange men were looking at her at school, which provoked a quick response.

Momma wanted to know who the men were and why they were studying her perfect little girl, all questions that the school director was at odds to explain. She in turn called Miss Christina into the meeting, where Momma told the teacher that she already knew all about her love affair with a man named Roy, with whom she was living and questioned why she was talking about such things with her little girl. Both Miss Christina and her supervisor were shocked. Miss Christina assured Momma that there had never been any conversation about her love life or living arrangements with her daughter and added that the little girl only talked to Roy twice, both times for less than a minute.

Momma was not convinced and told the pair that it was her intention to call the Bureau of Child Welfare and Health Department, as well as the State Education Office to report this unacceptable behavior, suggesting that the school was little more than a den of inequity. She abruptly ended the conversation by demanding that her daughter be brought to the office immediately and that she was withdrawing her from the school immediately.

After their departure, Miss Christina immediately called the university and reported the problems to her professor, who in turn advised the dean of the dilemma. Calls were quickly made to the appropriate agencies and a catastrophe was averted. But Miss Christina was still worried about Megan. What was to become of her. The professor agreed to reach out to Megan's parents to explain their concerns, but later reported that they refused to hear anything about the case study or the academics' concerns. Megan had dodged the bullet, so to speak and within a month was registered in a private elementary school run by a Catholic order of nuns near her home, safe from the prying eyes of do-good college types, her Momma would later say.

Megan in grade school was much like Megan in her pre-school environment; manipulative, unconcerned about her classmates and almost diabolically formulaic in her planning. She knew what the good sisters wanted and gave it to them in spades, the perfect child, with a dark side no one could see.

The next eight years were uneventful, at least on the surface, Megan continued to control everything around her zone of comfort, oblivious to anyone else's needs or feelings. She routinely bruised the psyches of her classmates and manipulated her teachers, but at least on the outside, her paper trail was spotless, without a demerit, detention or grade below an "A". She was the perfect student, the most beautiful girl in memory of every adult who had the honor to meet her and of course, she was the center of attention at every class function, from the annual picnic to the class play. She was always cast as the Virgin Mary in both the school Christmas pageant and the Passion Play at Easter and stood front row center for every school photograph.

Those eight years passed quickly and her departure into high school was none too soon. In fact, one of her teachers was very much aware that the beautiful 12 year old was showing signs of become sexually aggressive toward the older boys who played baseball after classes in the schoolyard, but declined to go on record about what she had witnessed. After all, it would not do to put a blemish on the school's most notable student, especially when the comment was based solely in the observations of one elderly nun. Megan, after all, was now bound for bigger and better things, a full scholarship to a prestigious prep-school adjacent to an Ivy League university.

Megan's home life has changed little since her days with Miss Christina, who was still vilified around the kitchen table by Momma, who by now had learned to blame anything unusual on her daughter's old teacher. She was the root of all evil, the person to be blamed when the first suggestion that Megan might be acting out over any number of things in the last eight years came up for a short discussion and never when she was at home. Megan was never the topic of anything negative when present, only discussions about how to put more of the household income into her clothing budget or how to pay for her cell phone was allowed in her presence.

Megan knew how to cover her tracks and turn any discussion to her own best interests. When Momma found a leafy substance in a small plastic bag in one of Megan's jackets, the child easily explained it presence by noting it was catnip for the old lady's feline next door. A single red pill in her jeans pocket was an allergy pill she was holding for a friend at a swim meet… the other girl couldn't chance getting it wet near the pool. Everything had a stock answer, there were no surprises where Megan was concerned. Every plan had a variety of escape clauses already thoroughly mapped out. Megan was still twenty years ahead of her time.

Her departure for prep school was heralded with a party equal to what some only could hope for on their wedding day, complete with the local newspaper photographer on hand and the mayor turning out to salute their small towns prize student, who had by this time amassed straight "A's" as well as trophies in swimming, girls basketball, track and as the youngest-ever winner of the local Miss Teen Beauty Pageant at age 13!

Prep school was to be Megan's biggest challenge ever to date. The school was immense in size as well as stature and Megan was sure that she would be going up against other kids her equal, unlike her experience with the local gentry, all of whom were dull by her standards in every way that mattered. Megan was actually shocked to find that while the student body at her new school was academically superior overall, none of them had what it would take to top her strategy for succeeding. While the girls were above average, both in looks and demeanor, all finishing school quality, they lacked the animal instinct that Megan had quietly cultivated to this point.

The boys on the other hand were more interesting. None of them were up to Megan's talents academically, at least none that she showed an interest in, but there were among that group a number of young men that raised her already aroused interests. Mind you, romance and relationships were of no concern to the budding Megan, but there was a simple animal instinct that needed to he serviced and she could see several candidates among her class to see to it she would not be otherwise obsessed with the hunt for gratification.

Academically, Megan excelled as always, and when stumped, she found that her male instructors were not unhappy to host an after class tutorial. While none were about to admit it, the young Miss Megan was more than just attractive, even at age 13 and her level of conversation was always pleasing. She was, as one instructor noted in her year book, "The perfect student!"

To consider giving Megan less than an "A" at this point was unthinkable, but unfortunately one female instructor in Megan's junior year Chemistry class attempted to do so. Apparently, Megan was devoting too much time to other pursuits and failed to turn in a lab paper in a timely fashion. When called on this oversight, Megan lost her normal cool and rather than attempting to purr her way through the impasse, she lashed out at her new nemesis, blurting out, "I'll give it to you when I am ready!"

The instructor took this easily, it was not uncommon for high achievers to lash out occasionally and there was a route to combat future outbursts. On the next quarterly report, Megan was shocked to find an "F" filed for an incomplete assignment, which dropped her overall grade in the class to an unheard of "B+" This was not acceptable and Megan was ready to wield her charms to have the decision reversed, first with the teacher herself, who off handedly rebuffed Megan's explanation and finally through channels to the head of the department.

Megan went into this meeting with a pat hand, an exceptional body of evidence to support her claim that she was in fact, the perfect student, but when asked to explain the missing assignment, Megan shocked everyone by first suggesting that her teacher had misplaced it and that it had been handed in on time, as usual and then added to the intrigue when she added that the teacher had some fictitious grievance against Megan and was attempting to ruin an otherwise perfect record.

The department head was somewhat unprepared for this frontal assault, expecting that Megan would ply a more enlightened response, throwing her fate to the mercy of the department chair. He in turn decided to refer the matter to a full academic review, noting that Megan was casting aspersions on a faculty member, which certainly would not do at this prestigious school. After all millionaires children had never tried this defense, so who was Megan to attempt it!

Megan was not expecting this response, she had always prevailed before with her full frontal approach to life and found the academic's response inappropriate. Never the less, she refused to apologize or recant her charge and agreed coolly to appear for the hearing before the department heads the following Monday. That gave her three days, the entire weekend to prepare.

Now the normally inapproachable Megan began to muster her forces, first enlisting the assistance of several of her drone male suitors, who in turn found some willing female students who would do anything to be part of Megan's entourage. A plan was hatched, groomed and perfected over that weekend and Megan entered the court of academic performance armed to the teeth. Knowing that no one on the faculty had ever seen this side of her or would be prepared to combat it.

Once the matter was read to the faculty in attendance, Megan was once again asked to repeat her allegations, which she did, this time with significant embellishment. In fact, no longer was Megan just saying that the instructor had misplaced her hard earned assignment report, and had some sort of ax to grind with her, but was prepared to bring forth a long line of students who were willing and ready to testify to similar misdeeds by the offending teacher and two who would testify that they had been approached by the woman for illicit purposes and then punished through the grade book when they rebuked the teacher's attention.

Megan had acquitted herself, coming out of a potential embarrassing situation by creating a tempest that was now threatening the offending teacher's very existence… and she was doing it without any feeling of remorse. Totally shocked by these new allegations, the faculty recessed to take the matter up with the academic dean and president of the school, who would naturally have to be advised of this very serious matter. The issue of Megan's grade was now a footnote to the proceedings and Megan, now tearfully, asked that they rescind the teacher's grade and remove the offending "F" from the grade book, which the now shocked department head did without question. Megan's straight "A" average was returned to order, which was her only concern. The fate of the teacher, the effect on the student body or on those who had conspired with her was of no interest to Megan, who was more than willing to reward those who had helped her, enlarging her entourage in the process.

In the end, the teacher in question took a paid leave from the school, there was no formal hearing on the allegations and eventually things returned to near normal except that no faculty member ever thought about giving Megan less than an "A" in any of her classes in her remaining year at the school. She was graduated with honors and voted most likely to succeed by her classmates. Those who actually knew her were divided into two camps, her faithful followers who existed to pick up the crumbs from her popular existence and her detractors who saw her for what she really was, but were too frightened to ever challenge her. Life was still very good for the most beautiful girl in the world.

As expected Megan was accepted to every university to which she applied, most with full scholarships, but her final choice of schools was something of a shock to everyone close to her. She chose a small college several states removed from her home and far away from the limelight everyone would have expected Megan to desire. When asked why she had chosen the school that she had, Megan smiled sweetly and noted with pride that the head of the psychology department at her new school was her former pre-school teacher, Miss Christina.

Megan's new school was intimate when compared to the physical size of her prep school, with fewer than a thousand students in total. The school was rated well and most graduates had no problem being accepted to good graduate schools, mostly in the field of psychology. Megan's application had flown through the application process without questions as one might expect of a straight "A" student from a prestigious prep academy. Miss Christina, now Dr. Christine Hewitt, Ph.D. was not aware of the application, nor should she have been, Megan after all was in the hands of the application committee just another high functioning high schooler finding her way to their college.

Megan's curiosity had been peaked however by an article she had found in a professional journal in her school library. It seemed that Christina Hewitt had taken her original notes on an unnamed pre-school student and devised a new battery of tests and procedures to identify a rare but significant set of anomalies. She had in fact made history with her dissertation and in the process made the unnamed little girl famous as well, an honor that was not lost on Megan.

On registration day, Megan came prepared with the courses she wished to take, but soon learned the lesson every freshman in college must learn, what one wants is not necessarily what one will get. Her biggest obstacle was the class she wanted most, Introduction to Psychology by Dr. Hewitt. She immediately took action and asked if she could request a meeting with the professor knowing that all instructors block out extra seats for their discretionary use. Her request was granted and she left registration to go to the psych center in the middle of her ivy covered campus.

Once at the center, she announced herself to the professor's secretary, who asked what she needed. She gave a terse response and the secretary said that she could handle that for her, but Megan insisted she needed to speak to the professor herself. Not caring one way or the other, the secretary rang the professor's line and announced there was a student wishing to see her. She was then directed to the chairman's office at the end of the corridor.

Miss Christina had not changed in Megan's eyes, still glowing with enthusiasm, a bright smile on her face as she welcomed the unknown freshman into her office.

"You really don't remember me?" Megan said almost saddened by the professor's lack of recognition. "It's me, Miss Christina, I'm Megan!"

"Princess," Dr. Hewitt shouted. "How wonderful to see you again. I am so glad to see you here. You're the one who needed an exemption for the Psych-1 class?"

"Yea, I guess you are pretty popular. I was in the gym at 8 a.m. sharp and it was already closed out," Megan sputtered in a very atypical fashion.

"Of course..." the professor said. "Always room for one of my favorite students!"

"I saw the article in *Psychology Today* about Student M. That was me, wasn't it," Megan asked, almost humbly.

"Yes, it was Megan. How do you feel about that," Dr. Hewitt asked.

"Well, you gotta do what you have to get along in this world, right. I mean there really wasn't anything negative about me. You got it all right. I'm a bit headstrong and all. I want what I want and I will get it." Megan answered.

"Well, we will talk more about that when you get settled into my class. I really am looking forward to your insights about all of that. I really am," the professor added.

"And I'm looking forward to learning more from you. You really taught me a lot, even back then. More from you than anyone else," Megan added as she headed for the door. "Gotta go and fight to get the rest of my classes."

As Megan ran from the room, Hewitt wondered just where this was all going. Did Megan actually choose a school based on the presence of her old pre-school teacher? And how had she changed. Hewitt allowed her mind to race for a moment. Maybe Megan had mellowed, or maybe there was a deeper meaning to her arriving at the college. Maybe, even a chance for a follow-up study on her most illustrious subject. She smiled. This was an interesting day, one way or the other.

Megan took on the system with her usual zeal, actually saying to a clerk at one point, "Hey, You don't know who I am. I'm a full scholarship kid here, not so lame freshman with a "C" average. Let's get things together, OK?" In the end, she got what she wanted, as always.

Life in the dorms would be another situation to deal with; Megan was scheduled to have a roommate, which would be a first for the American beauty. She enjoyed her space, but more important the dorm had an open access policy and Megan had no interest in anyone knowing the intimate details of her love life, which she intended to expand now that she was three states away from Momma. But how do you get rid of your assigned roomy?

Actually, it was simple enough for the beautiful Megan. Her roomy was attractive, but a bit introverted; a new freshman and the first time away from home. She had no siblings and had never lived with anyone else but her immediate family, so Megan decided to embarrass her into asking for a room reassignment. Within hours of her arrival, Megan took to walking around her new dorm room in nothing more than a thong. The space was cramped enough, but with Megan's choice of attire, the other young woman tended to try and hug the walls rather than have to come in contact with Megan's ample resources.

Often leaving the door open, the hall outside the room soon was swarming with young men and the scent of testosterone. While there were probably several coeds that could easily find an advantage to such behavior, it was not a good fit for Megan's roommate and the young woman asked for reassignment within 24 hours. Ironically, no one else asked to become the incoming freshman's new roomy and so Megan now had a two bed layout all to herself.

What Megan did not count on was just how fast the rumor mill could carry such antics over the campus and within the next 48 hours, Dr. Hewitt was also aware of the situation in the freshman dorm. She thought to herself that perhaps this was going to be a little more of a challenge than she first assumed, but never the less cracked a smile when she heard the tale, anyway. When asked at a freshman conference if this behavior needed to be addressed, she told her colleagues that it did not, "Come on guys, it's the 21st century, there is nothing going on over there we didn't already assume in the first place, just some first time away from home freshmen testing the waters!" The others nodded in agreement and the first confrontation with her young friend had been averted.

Meanwhile Megan was getting into the routine of the campus, up early for classes, the sometimes long runs from hall to hall, sometimes with short time periods for the sprint and then the attention of all the guys on campus who had already heard about the new freshman's proclivity for scant attire back in the dorm. To the guys, Megan was a rock star, to the girls, someone that attracted instant loathing with more negatives attached to her name than a church going person could ever dream of. For the first time in her life, Megan was attracting attention to herself in ways that were far from flattering and Dr. Hewitt wondered why.

One day, Megan walked into the women's rest room in the psych center and found a less than flattering caricature of herself in magic marker on a stall door. Under the drawing was a rather long essay.

"Once upon a time, there was a girl named Megan. She thought the world of herself. She was practically obsessed with herself and she was certainly in LOVE with herself. Wherever she went, whatever she was doing, she would always look into a mirror, just to gaze into her lustful, beautiful, self-obsessed face… but not for long!" the inscription said.

At first Megan was amused, then suddenly she felt another response, something foreign; she was feeling freight for the first time in her life. She ran from the room in tears and back to the dorm, where she ran into one of her dorm counselors, an attractive 30-something graduate student, who asked what was wrong. That after all was part of the job description, learn to overlook outrageous behavior and still be there for a student when they really needed it.

Megan told the counselor about the restroom art and paraphrased the message that was attached. The woman took a deep breath, giving herself time to review mentally everything she had learned thus far about counseling.

"Look Megan, there really are better things in life than always looking at yourself in the mirror and lets face it, you do that a lot. You project the feeling that no one is as good as you or as beautiful and you tend to make people feel that they are only around for your amusement or to act as your servants. This graffiti is a normal reaction from someone who just hates you because of who you project yourself to be. Id' prefer to think there is a better person inside you. Maybe you could try showing some respect for others and they will stop feeling how they seem to feel about you right now," the counselor offered.

Megan lowered her head for a moment in deep thought, then looked up with tears welling up in her eyes.

"Go to hell. You all feel that way because it is true. I am the most beautiful girl on campus. I can have any guy I want, take him from anyone I care to and I will always be on top. Screw you! You'll see. You'll all see!" she screamed as she left the room to return to her own space. On the door to her dorm room was a note.

"You're a bitch and you're ugly inside. Why don't you just leave?" the note said.

Megan read the note and then screamed at the top of her lungs. "Eat it bitches! None of you are any competition for me!"

Of course, life went on, classes had to be attended and even a princess in crisis has to perform. Megan had no problems attracting shallow boy toys by the dozen, each more handsome and muscularly sculpted than the next. She enjoyed parading them about campus, and at the dorm, where her antics often kept her dorm-mates awake at night, with screams and giggles galore from her room. Always the show off, she continued to leave her door open, as her already scanty attire seemed to shrink before a packed hallway. Life in the freshman dorm was becoming a living hell for everyone in residence, except for Megan who took pleasure in seeing other people squirm.

There were of course conferences, first with the dorm advisor, then the faculty advisor and even an impromptu board of inquiry, all to no end. To squash Megan's liberal interpretation of the campus rules might well upset the equilibrium of the entire school, so Megan continued on her merry, raucous way.

Classes of course were no problem for Megan, either. She certainly was bright enough to continue her collection of "A's" without any assistance, but then again, she now had a willing stable of boys who were more than willing to "help" with assignments, just for a chance to be closer to the precocious princess in her dorm room. It there was one thing more desirable than watching Megan from the hall of the dorm as she pranced around her room, it was being inside the room and possibly earning the right to have her sit on your lap for a moment as a thank you for a term paper well done.

All of this continued to wear thin with the rest of the coed community. Megan was single handedly tying up a goodly number of the available manpower on campus and was environmentally upsetting the delicate balance of natural selection in the process. Simply put, guys preferred to stroll over to the freshman dorm to catch a glimpse of Megan rather than go through the age old mating rituals with less than perfect, would be mates. The natural order was actually being upset.

None of this was lost on Professor Hewitt, who was attempting to keep a low profile while observing the goings on at the freshman dorm. To Hewitt, the entire affair was fascinating both anthropologically and psychologically. How one, nineteen year-old girl could upset an entire campus so effectively. She understood that this had to be a conscious plan, but pondered the question of why, exactly she had chosen this path. While others attempted to overlook all the game playing, Hewitt knew that this was a phenomenon to be studied in greater detail, and to that end, she eventually summoned her one time charge for a conference.

Christina Hewitt saw no reason to mix metaphors with Megan; she believed that both understood the reason for this meeting and when Megan arrived, five minutes before the scheduled get together, Hewitt cut right to the chase.

"Exactly what is going on, Megan," Hewitt asked the young beauty.

"Well, I'm not that popular on campus with the other girls and I think that is beginning to cause some problems," Megan offered.

"OK, well you and I have known each other for a lifetime, so I think I can talk to you directly, without all the niceties. You are upsetting nothing less than the academic and social balance of the campus and I believe you are doing it deliberately. My only question is why? Do you want my attention? Well, Megan, you certainly have it!"

Megan looked up with an earnest smile and seemed thoughtful for a moment. "Oh, no, it isn't your attention that I wanted. I knew I'd have that just by showing up at this school. No, I came here hoping that I could find a home and when I realized that I was hated from the first moment I arrived, well then I decided that I'd make them all pay," she spurted out.

"Megan, that is totally horrid. You can't make new friends by demanding their total obedience. What right do you think you have to ask that of people who don't know you?" Hewitt responded.

"Well, they should recognize that I am the most beautiful person on campus... well I am, aren't I? That's like a calling card. I am beautiful; guys will do anything just to be in reach of my scent. Can't they see that? I am beautiful, and smart, so why do they try to put me down?" Megan asked her old mentor.

"Because they have a life too, Megan. They have rights, those girls want to go to class, earn their grades, catch the eye of some boy they like and have their shot at romance. They don't want to have to bow to you for those privileges, Megan. They don't need your permission to exist and have their fun, too. Yes, it is true, you are probably the best looking girl on campus, but looks can only take you so far...."

Megan interrupts the professor, mid sentence. "What do you mean,' probably the best looking.' You know I am the best looking. I can have anyone I want...."

"No, Megan, that is not true. There are people on this campus who are in committed relationships. You might be able to turn their heads, but you can't really believe you can have all of them. Some people can look through you and see the real you."

Megan interrupts once again, "Yeah, sure. You know this because?"

"Because human nature tells me so. Love is not dependent on looks alone..." the professor begins to tell Megan, who once again had to interject her own read on the matter.

"You really think that I can't get any guy to dump his lover if I want him to? You are delusional. I can have anyone I want, right now. I always could, I always will. I am not like normal people. I don't get pimples; I attract men like flies to honey. I think you have to readjust your perspectives when you aim your little studies at me, Christina!" Megan says.

"OK first of all, you are not a case study, I think of you as a student I have known for a long time. Secondly, I'd appreciate you addressing me by my title, either doctor or professor, but not Christina. That is totally inappropriate in our relationship!" Dr. Hewitt demands.

"Go to hell," Megan replies. "Take that Ph.D. and shove it. You'd be no place without your little case study of 'Student M' and we both know it. I made you, you did nothing for me. But you will learn. You will….."

Now it was the professor's turn to interrupt.

"Megan, get yourself under control. I am trying to give you the best advice I can, if you can just put yourself in a neutral place for just a moment and stop the game playing…" Megan attempts to interrupt again, but Hewitt was not about to yield the floor. "Megan, you are beautiful and you are intelligent but you are also misguided and I am trying to tell you something about life before you go off headlong into a disaster. You can't continue on this path, it will destroy you. This isn't one of your Momma's soap operas on TV, this is real life. You looks will fade all too soon and if you don't get yourself together, you will have nothing!"

Megan takes a deep breath, "Yeah, right. Now I get it. You can't compete with me, so I should slow down so you can catch up, right. No way, Christina. You had your chance a long time ago. Remember the day at the fence at our old school yard. I was a baby and I could have had your boyfriend. Face it, you can't compete with me. I'm better than you, always have been, always will be!' Its been nice chatting with you… If you need any help with part two of you case study, just ask, I'd be happy to cooperate for old time's sake. Just don't get in the way, Christina, you really can't hope to compete!"

Megan got up, with a swish of her short skirt and was out the door before Dr. Hewitt could utter another word. In fact, Hewitt was simply without words; she had hoped to learn what was on her old pupil's mind, and now she knew. She didn't fully understand, but she had been told. What would happen next was the only unanswered question.

While Megan had put up a strong front when confronting Dr. Hewitt, the confrontation was not without its effect. Megan retreated to her dorm room and for the first time closed the door behind her, leaving a 'do not disturb' sign on the handle of the now-famous door. She was tired, exhausted really and needed a short nap, she undressed and climbed between the sheets after closing the blinds to her room, which was also totally out of character.

Sleep came almost instantly. A deep sleep, but not restful by any means. Megan began to dream, which was not normal for the princess. She woke several hours later, her sheets soaked in perspiration. She remembered nothing of her dreams, but knew she had dreamed. She got out of bed, it was now almost 3 a.m. and walked out into the hall toward the common showers, attired in her normal dorm garb, an almost nothing red satin thong. As she entered, another girl was exiting the shower room wearing an oversized terrycloth robe, there was a passing glance and then a muffled utterance, "Slut!" which Megan chose to ignore. She walked into the shower, stepping out of her thong and allowed the warm water to massage her still weary body, then stepping into the adjacent room she began to towel off, in front of a mirror.

At first, nothing seemed unusual. Even though the mirror was slightly fogged by the humid air of the room, Megan could see her form in the reflection, her perky breasts, and perfect posterior, her long mane falling off her shoulders and carefully cropped other patch, seemed in order. She stopped for a moment to take in her own beauty and then returned to her nightly rituals, but once up close to the reflective surface, she began to notice things… little things, a line, a crease and unruly hair. She was not happy with imperfection but was tired and decided quickly that all of the stresses of the last few weeks were taking a toll. She resolved to do something about all of that in the morning and returned to her room, where she quickly pulled the damp sheet from her bed and loosely fitted a new set in their place before collapsing back under them.

If the morning alarm had rung, Megan was surely not aware of it. Once again, she rose from her bed in mid-morning and noting the time muttered, "Damn," when she realized that she has slept through her morning 'Critical Thinking' class. She looked down at herself as she rose and noticed something very unusual, what almost looked like a crease across her belly. She hesitated for a moment and looked again. She could see her belly button ring, but then there seemed to be a never before present bulge… she could not see her own pubic hair as she looked down. Impossible as it seemed, it had to be an optical illusion, but Megan appeared to have grown a belly over night. She ran to the closet door and flung it open to reveal a full length mirror inside. She gazed intently at her own reflection. "Oh my God!" she uttered. The young woman in the mirror had a pronounced pouch, not totally unattractive, but not Megan at all.

She looked harder, squinting to see every detail. The belly button ring was her's, but the body was definitely not. Her pubic area was bushy, there was that slight belly to contend with and her breast, "Oh my god," Megan heard herself utter again. Her once perky breasts were now sagging! There was a pronounced crease at her neckline and then the face. "Oh my God, my God, my God," Megan repeated. It was Megan's face all right, but not the face of a 19 year-old; there were lines and subtle creases around the eyes and forehead. "Oh my God," she muttered once again.

Panic was quickly growing within her. What was this? Some wasting disease? What are all those vertical lines on her stomach? "Oh my God," she muttered even more loudly this time. "Stretch marks!" Megan quickly contemplated her options; should she run to the campus medical station? No, then everyone would know; an off campus doctor would be a better choice, but how to get there. "I can't walk out in public looking like this for everyone to see," Megan said out loud to herself. For the first time in her life Megan wished she had one true friend to confide in at this moment, but that after all was impossible.

Megan grabbed a too short robe from the closet and went back to her bed, sitting up in a fetal ball for what seemed like forever, trying desperately to regain enough composure to think things through rationally, but rational thought was eluding her at the moment, panic had truly set in. Several times she returned to the mirror, each time noticing something new. Her perfect posterior was sagging noticeably now, her legs seemed to be getting pudgy and there was hair sprouting everywhere, even one, it appeared on the tip of her once chiseled chin. Her face was becoming round and there were blotches on her body. Surely this was some fatal disease!

Megan tried to go back to sleep, possibly to dream but such a solution was not easily obtained. She tossed and turned, stopping periodically to return to her mirror to see even more imperfections on each passing glance. Finally she slammed the closet door shut. At one point she had to go to the bathroom; as she sat on the toilet an unexpected release of gas echoed in the small room, which immediately filled with the scent of sulfur. "Oh, my God!" Megan shouted. She had never been plagued by flatulence in her life and had no way of knowing what the ungodly smell was from. She returned to bed, praying for a quick end to her misery. Death at this point was preferable to the life she was seeing unfold before her. The girl who was once the most beautiful in the entire world was now unable to control her bodily functions and was being transformed into a hideous monster before her very eyes.

How could this be? What was happening? Megan was filled with questions but no real answers. She was a prisoner in a body she now detested, her world and her life could no longer be as before. She was doomed. Who could she turn to for help. She didn't really know a single girl on campus and she certainly did not enjoy a relationship with any man she could talk to about her utter transformation. She heard herself talking, but didn't even recognize the voice, even that had been transformed into a deep, guttural tone.

The though of suicide entered her mind, but even the thought of such a hideous body being found in the beautiful Megan's room, was more than she could reconcile. Perhaps she could escape from the dorm late at night and disappear, and then, should she decide to end her life, no one would know that the unrecognizable body was her's and at least a legend might arise from her ashes about the once great beauty that suddenly disappeared one lonely night, never to be heard of again. Somehow that appealed to this afflicted young woman; at least in death she would continued to be a great beauty.

Yes, that was a plan she thought. But now her plan was interrupted by a more physically pressing problem. She was beginning to itch in the most embarrassing places and the need to scratch was uncontrollable, no matter how degrading. Megan could not remember a single moment in her life when she had even touched her own behind, never mind deal with an uncontrollable need to place one of her own fingers there, the affliction quickly spread, both north and south of her midline and a few minutes later Megan realized that she was facing additional insult to her already momentous injuries; she was getting her period with a flow she had never dreamed possible. "Oh, my God!" she said in near hysteria, she began to tear her closet apart. She did not have a single sanitary appliance in the room, nothing, but toilet paper, which would be difficult to keep in place, given the fact that the once beautiful Megan did not own a single pair of conventional underwear!

Megan had never had a very strong flow to begin with, her periods were totally predictable, lasting three days and requiring a total of nine tampons. Cramping was never an issue for her in the past, the words pain and period had no connection for this perfect creature. Now she was in outrageous pain and didn't know what to do.

Unable to escape her room, she was faced with the greatest dilemma of her young life. Placing her future in the hands of fate, she decided to call for help! Her only real choice was, of course, Dr. Hewitt. She sat crossed legged, with the phone in resting on her legs. She looked down, about to dial but then noticed something new, yet again. She jumped from the bed, a wad of toilet paper between her legs and waddled over to the closet. Opening the door once more, she looked in utter disbelief. She no longer had a waistline, she heard her new, gruff voice exclaim, "Oh God, I'm morphing into a pear!" No, she though after a moment, "I look just like Momma!"

Returning to her bed, tears pouring from her eyes, she quickly punched in the number for the psych center and Dr. Hewitt. At first the professor's secretary refused to forward the call, not recognizing Megan's new voice, but finally took pity on the tearful caller at the other end of the line. Hewitt answered quickly, "Who is this," she asked in disbelief when she was told that Megan was on the phone, but did not recognizing the voice.

"It's me, honest. I need your help…please," the gruff voice said.

"Who is this?" Hewitt asked once again.

"It's me, Megan, something terrible has happened, I'm at the dorm, I need you to come over here," she continued.

"OK, calm down. Come right over and we will talk," Hewitt responded, not being totally sure who she was talking to.

"No, I can't go out. You don't understand. You have to come…."

Hewitt recognized total panic in the caller's voice and once again asked for some confirmation of the caller's identity. Megan reiterated the urgency of her call and begged Hewitt to come. Finally, she agreed and Megan hung up. A moment later the phone rang again in Megan's room, which she promptly answered. It was Hewitt, reconfirming that it had actually been Megan calling.

"Megan, I don't understand. What's happening?" Hewitt asked.

"I can't explain on the phone, please, come here…" the gruff voice pleaded.

While Hewitt was not convinced the caller was actually Megan, she was convinced that whoever the caller was, she was in crisis. She grabbed her coat and proceeded across campus to the freshman dorm, mounting the stairs two at a time to the second floor and to the locked door she knew was Megan's. She knocked and the door swung open, but she did not see anyone. She walked in carefully, to find Megan bent over in pain behind the door.

"What's happened to you?" was Hewitt's natural reaction.

Megan made her way back to the bed, stumbling as she went.

"I don't know," was her response to Hewitt's question.

Hewitt walked closer to the young woman, and raised her bowed head toward the single light in the room. Megan's eyes were swollen from hours of crying, she was Hewitt would note later in her journal, a wreck.

"Have you taken any drugs?" Hewitt asked. Megan shook her head negatively. "Have you been drinking?"

"No nothing like that. I went to sleep and woke up like this?" Megan explained tearfully.

Hewitt noted the flow of blood from between her Megan's legs and the soaked clump of toilet paper. She reached into her bag and produced a tampon, placing it in the girl's hand. "You do know how to use one of these," she asked.

"Yes, of course, but I didn't have any!" Megan muttered.

"OK. Lets get you into the bathroom and clean you up," Hewitt suggested.

Megan complied lowly.

"Honey, you have to go and get a quick shower," Hewitt told Megan as she walked slowly into the bathroom.

Megan relied, "No, I can't do that. I don't want anyone to see me like this."

Hewitt shook her head in agreement and picked up the phone, dialing the dorm counselors room.

"This is Dr. Hewitt. How many students are supposed to be on the floor right now?" she asked the grad student in charge of the freshman dorm.

"OK. I want you to sound the dorm bells and clear the hallways for a few minutes for me, if anyone asks, just say it s Homeland Security Drill. I'll dial your cell when I want you to let the kids back in, OK? Good!"

A moment later the bells did ring and the few students left in the dorm filed from the building, most disbursing to the nearby student union building. Hewitt then escorted Megan to the showers and back to her room without anyone seeing her.

Once the pair were safely back in the room, Hewitt advised the counselor that the drill was complete and thanked her for her cooperation. She then told Megan to dress in something comfortable, while she made her prize student bed.

"Now Megan. I think we need to do a little work together. OK? I need you come over here, lay down and just relax," Hewitt directed.

Megan was too exhausted to question her mentor's directions.

"OK, now I want to place you in a little hypnotic state, nothing too extreme, I just need you to be more relaxed, OK." Megan shook her head in agreement.

Within a minute Megan was deep under the hypnotic control of her mentor and Hewitt set about to calm the young woman, relieving her of the stress that was all around her, reassuring her that everything would be alright. Megan would remember none of this and Hewitt was still not sure what had transpired that evening, but she knew that if she was to help Megan, she first had to get her back under control. Within a half hour, Megan was once again awake and feeling refreshed, but soon was back on a track toward total hysteria until Hewitt used a post hypnotic suggestion to once again calm the girl. Once under control Hewitt explain to Megan that she needed her to go back and recall, calmly what had brought on this hysteria. Megan once again nodded in the affirmative.

Over the next two hours Megan retold the tale of waking to a new, ever expanding body, the growth of hair, the itching and scratching, the bloating, flatulence, and pain, not to mention her now un-Godly menstrual cramps. She was constantly crying softly now, her eyes swollen and red as she recounted the horror of being trapped in her dorm room, without friends to assist her.

Hewitt suggested that perhaps Megan could recall the dream that she had wakened from the evening before, when she first had to run to the shower drenched in sweat. At first Megan said softly that she could not recall, but then with the assistance of another post hypnotic suggestion, she lapsed into a restful sleep and began to talk aloud about the dream, every word of which Hewitt was recording for the files. Megan's memory was of a shadow figure, who was warning her about the evils attached to being too vain. She continued on for some time, recalling past memories through the help of this shadow figure.

Once again awake, Megan did not remember what she had relived in that dream and calmer, she asked Hewitt if she could help her to find a hospital where some cure might be found for her ailments. Megan was shocked when she turned to see Hewitt smiling. Was she so pleased with her young charges afflictions. Megan said nothing, turning inward in thought. Perhaps it was only fitting for Hewitt to smile, she was sure everyone would be happy with this turn of events, after all.

"Honey, relax. Everything is going to be just fine," Hewitt said in hopes of reassuring her charge. "Honest, you can relax now."

Megan, exhausted from her ordeal and resigned to her fate, simply asked that Hewitt stay with her and once that promise was given, she fell into a deep cleansing sleep.

The long morning turned to afternoon and into early evening. Hewitt called her office for them to bring in some food and a more comfortable set of clothes, keeping her promise not to leave Megan's side as she slept on. It was two in the morning before Megan woke again. Hewitt offered her a glass of juice as the young woman crawled up into a fetal like sitting position on the side of the bed.

"What will happen to me now?" Megan asked Hewitt.

"What will happen?" Hewitt responded.

"Where will I go, what will I do, is there any hope that we can find a doctor or hospital that can help me?" the girl asked in a breaking voice.

"Megan, you don't need any help. Maybe a little therapy to get you to work through some of your issues, but there is nothing physically wrong with you that I can see." Hewitt finally responded after a long, contemplative pause.

"But how did this happen to me so suddenly. I mean, one moment I was normal, the next I was a mess," Megan protested softly.

"Megan, there is nothing wrong," Hewitt repeated.

"Yeah, OK, I'm not dieing, but my whole life has to change. I doubt I can even fit into my jeans anymore," Megan began to ramble.

Hewitt stopped her mid-sentence with a gentle finger to her lips.

She then took Megan's hand and beckoned her to rise from her bed and over to the closet door. Megan at first was repelled by the thought of looking at her disfigured self, but then quickly resigned herself to the inevitable. Here was the once beautiful Princess Megan, a girl who could spend hours admiring herself in the mirror, now trembling at the thought of seeing her image once again.

The door opened and Megan took a quick glance, then a longer look and finally began to stare intently at her image in the mirror.

What Megan saw was a miracle. Granted her hair was not in place and she had no makeup on, but through the looking glass appeared the Princess once more, in all her beauty. Her shape, her perfect figure, her perfect body, the face that could launch a thousand ships had miraculously returned. But how?

"I don't get it. I don't understand. What happened?" Megan asked.

"Well, it is going to take a little work of course, but my best guess was pure hysteria. You were so unhappy with your life you subconsciously wanted to change it at any cost, but you didn't know how. You see, Subject M was always conflicted. She looked at her parents and could not reconcile where she had come from, but she sublimated all of that under the façade of a perfect human being, beautiful, bright, articulate, even at age four.

"You've lived with that you entire life. You subconsciously wanted to know the answer to that one question, but over the years the "beautiful" you kept sweeping that under the rug. You were obsessed with being the best, the prettiest, the brightest, the perfect girl, but once you obtained it, the question kept knocking at your mind's door but you were too scared to answer it," Hewitt attempted to explain. "You were always a good kid at heart, but you had to keep up appearances. If you didn't, the questions would naturally come through and you weren't ready to handle that."

"But what happened yesterday to change all that,' Megan asked stoically.

"Well, my educated guess is that you menstrual cycle was always very light. But as your body matures, some things change. Subconsciously, your head knew that something different was about to happen and it prepared for the worst. Your hormones were raging at full tilt and your conscious mind was not prepared for it.

"You went to sleep that evening exhausted from all of this and you dreamed. And you dreamed about all those unanswered questions, but when you woke, your conscious mind didn't know how to process all that new information. You saw your parents as imperfect, not attractive, not all that bright and you rationalized that because of those facts, you were destined to become the same. You woke, the information got mixed with that rush of hormones and you lapsed into nothing less than a full psychotic episode. You saw yourself as you believed you truly had to be, from the Princess to Shrek in one short hour. You cried, your voice became hoarse, you began to bleed and manifested all of your worst fears, causing rashes and pain. You looked in the mirror, the one place that you had always found your reality and this time saw what you believed you had to become. But it was all in your head, honey. You can relax now. It was a dream. Honest!" Dr. Hewitt concluded.

Megan slowly shook her head in agreement.

"But…" Megan said softly. "But, what do I do now? I mean, I am the Princess of Bitchiness. No one wants to be my friend. I couldn't buy a room mate if I had a million dollars. I want friends, people to talk to, not to use. I've been so wrong, for so long. What do I do?"

"It's OK baby, It will all be OK, now…" Hewitt said to her charge. "You can make changes. No one is going to accept the change over night, you will have to make a real effort to show you want to be different, it will take some time, and maybe a little therapy, but honest, by next semester, you will be one of the girls. Honest!"

Megan was tired again and asked if Hewitt would spend the night. Dr. Hewitt agreed and turned to the other bed in the room. The next morning, Megan got up, and went to the showers, this time in a bathrobe. She greeted everyone she knew by name and then returned to her room to dress.

"I have to get to my office Megan. I put my cell phone number by your cell. Call me if you need anything, OK?" Dr. Hewitt said.

"OK, I will. I'll take it one step at a time, I promise. I'll make it all work out," Megan exclaimed as the pair left the dorm room together, Megan to her classes and the professor to her office.

In class, Megan found things rough-going at first, but she managed to reach out and the healing process had begun.

In her office, Dr. Hewitt was sitting at her computer. She told her secretary that she was not to be disturbed and closed her inner office door. She began to type.

Update on Subject M.

The subject has completed the expected transformation, without undue effect. The experiment is completely successful. I am extremely pleased with these accomplishments as well as my genetic part in the process.

After nearly twenty years of research and experimentation the subject has awakened from her post hypnotic suggestive state as concluded in earlier tests within the MK Ultra Project. She still has no idea of her lineage, or who her real mother might be or that she is a hybrid human or that she has been part of this government project, but field results now suggest that she is the perfect human, as we expected. We will keep her under surveillance for some time to come to be sure the transformation is complete, but is reasonable to suggest that the superiors can now be informed that, "the butterfly has begun to spread her wings."

Christina M. Hewitt, Ph.D.
Project Director

Post script: You might suggest that the male subject currently under testing at the Nevada site, be conditioned to meet his intended mate in the foreseeable future. I am prepared to make arrangements to have him registered as an exchange student and make the necessary introduction between "The Princess" and "The Prince" as soon as possible.

CMH